T0248433

LIFE
ON
EARTH

ALSO BY DORIANNE LAUX

Only as the Day Is Long: New and Selected Poems

The Book of Men

Facts about the Moon

Smoke

What We Carry

Awake

The Poet's Companion: A Guide to the Pleasures of Writing Poetry
(with Kim Addonizio)

LIFE

ON

EARTH

Poems

DORIANNE LAUX

W. W. NORTON & COMPANY
Independent Publishers Since 1923

For information about permission to reproduce selections from this book, write to Permissions, W. W. Norton & Company, Inc., 500 Fifth Avenue, New York, NY 10110

For information about special discounts for bulk purchases, please contact W. W. Norton Special Sales at specialsales@wwnorton.com or 800-233-4830

Manufacturing by Versa Press

Production manager: Louise Mattarelliano

ISBN 978-1-324-06582-1

W. W. Norton & Company, Inc., 500 Fifth Avenue, New York, N.Y. 10110
www.wwnorton.com

W. W. Norton & Company Ltd., 15 Carlisle Street, London W1D 3BS

1 2 3 4 5 6 7 8 9 0

I began writing because I had made friends with the dead: they had written to me, in their books, about life on earth, and I wanted to write back and say "yes, house, bridge, river, hair, no, maybe, never, forever."—Mary Ruefle

Contents

LIFE
ON
EARTH

IN ANY EVENT

If we are fractured
we are fractured
like stars
bred to shine
in every direction,
through any dimension,
billions of years
since and hence.

I shall not lament
the human, not yet.
There is something
more to come, our hearts
a gold mine
not yet plumbed,
an uncharted sea.

Nothing is gone forever.
If we came from dust
and will return to dust
then we can find our way
into anything.
What we are capable of
is not yet known,
and I praise us now,
in advance.

—for us

Spirit Level

"When making an axe handle
the pattern is not far off."
　　　　　　—Gary Snyder

My mother was either horizontal on the couch,
or vertical, a plumb line from her spine
to the top of her head to the ceiling that spins
when she drinks, alcohol and an air bubble
trapped, sealed and fixed inside her, her face
carved from wood, a tear gliding slowly
down the curve of her cheek. My mother
was once a spirit in this world. Once
she breathed for me, above me, beside me,
behind me. Now I feel her warm breath
on my neck summer nights, peering
over my shoulder as I write every poem, whispering
Let me in. I let her in. I remember every time
she picked me up or set me down, put me
to bed or woke me from dreams, and now
I see how my whole life has been a dream,
one she built for me from the ground up,
her daughter, my mother the axe, beautiful
tool with which she shaped me, a house
much like the one she lived in, but smaller,
fewer rooms, a tiny unusable attic
and a cluttered basement. I let her in,
like she let me in. She became my carpenter,
stone mason and bricklayer, piling me up
cell by cell, the blade that shaped my legs,
my arms, my surveyor, millwright.
She used herself as a template, her genes
tough, her organs elastic, her eyes and nose,

forehead and mouth. And when her body
from which my body was made
was slipped into the hot retort, I burned
too. She refused the beveled casket,
the oiled mahogany box, last drawer
for the dead, wanted only the fury
of fire, the blue-white flames unmaking her
with their licking tongues, house
her grandmother built, and her grandmother
before her, all of them giving what they
had been given, the hardwood floors,
staircases and banisters, their deepest
cupboards, their heavy doors flung wide
so the breeze I would be could blow through.

Salt

Since the beginning, salt.
Seawater we climbed out of, what
would later fall from our eyes
when we saw the yellow bells
of Datura, confusion of moonflowers
hanging over our shoulders
as we roamed the new earth.

The beaten roads to the mines
we pulled it from in wooden carts,
crystalline in sun, shipped
on the flanks of barges across
the blue Mediterranean, the answer
to preserving food, tanning hides,
bleaching pulp, 14,000 uses
for the fine grains we pinch
into the pot, how much, how little
depends on the tongue. Jewels
of salt sewn into the hems
of winter coats, strewn
on icy streets. The Salton Sea
creeping through the Imperial Valley,
the nothing of the Colorado Desert.

Table salt, rock salt, kosher salt,
Himalayan Pink, Celtic Sea,
Fleur de sel hand-harvested
from the tidal pools of France.
Flake salt, black and red Hawaiian salt,
smoked salt, pickling salt,
the potato chip and the lowly pretzel,
bread crust, cold cuts, nuts, the beads
of sweat we lick from our upper lip,

rub between our damp, nervous
palms, and in the end poured in rings
around the dead to keep insects
from feasting on our flesh.

The Thermopolium

Ancient Snack Stall Uncovered in Pompeii.
—The Daily Star

Even in 79 AD, people loved street food,
all the young Romans flocking around
the sizzling terracotta pots, the stalls frescoed
with chickens and hanging ducks, hot drinks
served in ceramic two-handled pateras
filled with warm wine and spices.
Their sandaled feet glimmered
as they milled around, waving hellos,
smudging one another's cheeks
with kisses, murmuring gossip,
complaining about the crazy rise
in the price of wheat. Soups and stews,
skewered meats, stacks of flatbread,
honey cakes and candy made with figs.
They sprawled on the steps or sat
near a neighbor's open door, stood
under a blur of windows, someone
playing a lyre, barefoot children
singing the Ode of Horace. Just like
New York before the pandemic,
before the many retreated and retired
to their living rooms to watch the news
on a loop, alone with a cat or dog,
a furry stay against the nothing,
nothing, nothing of loneliness,
their dreams a passport to fear.
I used to see the excavated people
of Pompeii, frozen in time, caught
curled in sleep or kneeling, a couple

fucking, though there is one
of a possible father propped
in what looks like an easy chair,
a mother bouncing a child
on her lap, as if they'd decided
in their final moments to be
happy, to go into the afterlife
covered in ash, buried alive
by joy.

I'll Be Here on My Back Porch

—*for Thelma and Louise*

Tonight the sky is pulling its endless wagon of stars
across a canvas of cracked black paint, the constellations

falling into place: bear, harp, Job's Coffin. Job who died
old and full of days. And though he suffered senselessly

in the final chapter he gets his wife, his children, the land
he tended back. The original happy ending. And what

of our world's suffering? Descendants of Job, the doors
of our workplaces chained, locked, our families sick

and dying, our lives lived alone, drowning in obscurity.
Will we find and name a new constellation after the virus?

The Contagion Constellation? The Corona Dusk? I suppose
I began to miss the movies first, gathering in the dark,

my shoulders brushing up against my animal kind,
all of us exchanging breath, our strangers' hearts beating

as one heart as the huge women on screen clasped hands
and drove off the edge of the Grand Canyon. And with a last

kiss the canvas backdrop turns white, the camera's aperture
narrowing, the house lights coming up, a herd of souls walking

toward the open doors who had all seen the same thing, scene
after scene, laughing our herd laughter, crying our hard human tears.

Psalm

There are creatures in the understory,
snails with whorled backs and silver boots,
trails beetles weave in grass, black rivers
of ants, unbound ladybugs opening their wings,

spotted veils and flame, untamed choirs

of banjo-colored crickets and stained glass cicadas.
How shall we count the snakes and frogs
and moths? How shall we love the hidden
and small? Mushrooms beneath leaves

constructing their death domes in silence,

their silken gills and mycelial threads, cap scales
and patches, their warts and pores. And the buried
bulbs that will bloom in spring, pregnant with flower
and leaf, sing Prepare for My Radiance, Prepare

for the Pageantry of My Inevitable Surprise.

These are the queendoms, the spines and horns,
the clustered hearts beating beneath our feet.
Though the earth is locked in irons of ice and snow
there are angels in the undergrowth, praise them.

Ode to the Territory

I've taken my country for granted,
its morning songs breaking
over the craggy backs of mountains,
its violet gloves of rain, its frayed fields of corn.
I saw it as nothing more than a long road
drawn through scrub and sand, carved
into hillsides, silver bridge over a river
licking its own mossed banks—
its silos and windows, its silage and slag.
I took it for granted the way a man
takes a plate of buttered potatoes
from a woman's troubled hands, clean
socks from a drawer, sheets
smelling of wind. The way a man
curls his fingers around a woman's
thin wrist and follows her, unafraid,
into the woods. The way a child
opens her arms, her wings, his eyes,
his mouth, like a bird, expecting
to be fed. O wheelbarrows
filled with red earth, O horses
threshing the meadow's yellow weeds,
O ponds and geese and cracked
dinner bells, O sparks like stars
flung from the trains' metal wheels
winding, unbroken, past backyards
and junkyards, O expanse, O oceans
lapping, O coastlines' jagged boulders
holding in the sea, gulls turning above you,
the tin ceiling of night falling to its knees.

The Optimism of French Toast

No matter how many years since
the first bite passed my lips, that business
of eggs and day-old bread, ribbon of syrup,
fireflies of butter sparking my tongue's buds,
I think of my Acadian ancestors
landing on the shores of Nova Scotia, dragging
logs from the deep woods, fashioning windows,
hanging laundry from two oars dug into sand—
the flags of domesticity flayed by the wind.
I see the fruits of their labor rise up
from the marshes: beets, parsnips, cabbages
and corn, and the wheat they ground
to powder and baked into bread.
And the chickens shook out egg after egg
we broke into shallow bowls, beat
with a spoon, each thick slice dipped
into that loom of albumen, chalazae and yolk,
then laid on a scrim of grease in the pan
where it sizzled its solitary song.
How could these French be
considered a scourge, their houses
burned to the ground they had worked,
forced to take the tangled circuitry
of dirt roads with nothing but what
they could carry on their backs? No time
for funerals, no place to go. And yet
here I am at my kitchen table listening
to Clifton Chenier on the radio, daughter
of a people who refused to die: sacks
of wheat on their shoulders, spoon
in a belt loop, sugar sprinkled in a pant cuff,
a sleeping chicken hidden under a coat.

Third Rock from the Sun

That streetlight looks like the slicked backbone
          of a dead tree in the rain, its amber lamp blazing
like the first neon fig glowing in the first garden
          on a continent that split away from Africa
from which floated away Brazil. Why are we not

          more amazed by the constellations, all those flung
stars held together by the thinnest filaments
          of our evolved, image making brains. For instance,
here we are in the middle of another Autumn,
          plummeting through a universe that made us

from its shattering and dust, stooping
          now to pluck an orange leaf from the sidewalk,
a small veined hand we hold in an open palm
          as we walk through the park on a weekend we
invented so we would have time to spare. Time,

          another idea we devised so the days would have
an epilogue, precise, unwavering, a pendulum
          strung above our heads. When was the sun
enough? The moon with its diminishing face?
          The sea with its nets of fish? The meadow's

yellow baskets of grain? If I were in charge
          I'd say leave them there on their backs
in the grass, wondering, eating berries,
          rolling toward each other's naked bodies
for warmth, for something we've yet to name,

when the leaves were turning colors in their dying
and we didn't know why, or that they would return,
       bud and green. One of a billion
small miracles. This planet will again be stone.

Winter Brother

These nights I walk out and look up
at Orion, my winter brother, spellbound
each time I trace him to wholeness
from the star on his right shoulder to the star
on his left, down to form his torso,
lower down, his little skirt.
I know his right hand holds a club
but I replace it with two splayed arrows
pointing up, in his left a lion's pelt
that for me becomes a bow.
From hunter to archer, just like that.
And why not? Whoever made him up
is lost to history's shimmering distance,
and I'm here now in my dark backyard,
a splash of ghost-sibling lilies
glowing at my feet. I like to think
he's my older brother
who died far from home
on a lonely road, his broken body
found in a muddy gutter
swollen with rain. That's how it is
down here on the death-packed earth
where nothing is eternal, the bodies
buried haunch to haunch
beneath the indifferent dirt.
I remember his handwriting
on a postcard, the lines squashed
between the address and the card's
cut edge. *I miss you. I love you.*
I saw some sights today
you wouldn't believe.
On the other side a wall
of etched bricks, a statue

of Karl Marx's fat head, his beard
of gray stone. When he died
I felt alone, some part of me
went cold, some echo
following me like a false star,
so I lifted my brother
into the sky where I could ride
on his belt as he strode over
the seven continents, sharing
an eyedropper of water between us.

Bisquick

My mother could whip
anything up from a box
of the stuff, a casserole,
a cobbler, Mississippi
Pot Roast with cheese biscuits,
chicken and dumplings
or fried chicken, the skin
crispy as her cookies and pie crust.
It seemed the oven was always on,
the dial pointing to home
where we'd run back to
from wherever we had
gotten to, leaving footprints
on her clean floor, mud or sand
or the water that thundered
from the hose in summer.
She served the silky gravy
in a scratched glass boat,
poured like good fortune
over our mashed potatoes,
all of us having dug out
our wonder craters to receive it.
And sometimes I came home
early just to smell the air
scented with mingled
spices, see the banners
of flour the pan left
on the counter when she lifted it,
the bottom blackened by years
of burned butter. We'd wake
to pancakes in the cast iron skillet,
and it seemed she'd never slept,
never stopped, eggs cracking open,

spilling each whole yellow globe
into a blue bowl. What were we
waiting for but to see her
at the sink, her long bare feet
on the cool tiles, just
an ordinary woman
made of flint and roses,
her black hair tied back
with a drugstore scarf.

Singer

If I could go back to the living room window
of my childhood house, look again
through the pane, it would be a telescope lens
through which I might see the first woman
I ever met, my mother at her sewing machine,
rewinding the bobbin, little spool with holes
like an old movie reel our tiny lives
spun inside of. I might see
her long piano fingers touch the balance wheel,
the throat plate, the presser bar, one bare foot
working the treadle, her heel revealing
only the first three letters in black latticed metal:
SIN. My mother was what some called
a sinful woman: divorced, pregnant
without a husband, a baby boy given up
for adoption, remarried, another baby
born of another man, a one night stand,
while her husband was away at war.
She drank too much, thought too much,
laughed with her head thrown back, danced
with anyone. Too pretty, too brainy,
too tall, her black hair a snare
that hooked men in. But right now
she's fully visible, stretching the fabric
for a kitchen curtain, a child's dress,
swatches she salvaged from the deep
sale bins, using the selvedge for a hem
thereby cutting her handwork by half,
the black oiled mechanism banging out
dress after dress, tablecloths and runners,
nothing she couldn't cobble together
from the waste of others. She was
a very particular, peculiar mother

and by now you can see why
we loved her. She was a lit fuse
in the rain. She turned from her work
and set those same fingers
on the piano keys and pulled
music through the air. Making something
from nothing was what she was good at:
love, children, pants and skirts
to dress them in, a table covered
with cherries on which the beautiful food
appeared, roses from her front yard garden
in an old cracked vase, her long arms
around our shoulders saying *Sit still. Eat.*
Try not to spill anything.

In Praise of WD-40

I have never been without a can
        of its water displacing spray, born
one year after my own birth, 1953,
        by the Rocket Chemical Company,
a trade secret never patented,
        inducted into the Air and Space
Museum in San Diego where
        I grew up surrounded by
the conjoining of metal and rust:
        squeaky screen doors, stuck
drawers, a lock fevered
        with rust, bolts and screws
that would not come loose,
        embedded like stones
in a striker plate. I love the handy
        familiarity of its
American blue can with the yellow
        half oval, its thin red
"smart straw" for those hard
        to reach places,
the aerosol sound it makes
        as it swishes away the worst
in a haze of hydrofluorocarbons.
        I like the feel of my thumb
on its trigger, the way
        it releases the caught cogs
of the world, as if it could loose
        the hinge of the hurt hawk's wing,
the clamped closed jaw
        of the garter snake, unfasten
the fuchsia petals
        so they could open

over the tongues of their bells and ring
      their summer-baffled songs,
slough off the shingles
      from the eyes of angels
so they may better see us
      in the dark, carting our coal-bucket
dreams or weeping like willows
      at the river's ruffled edge.
It was the answer to everything:
      releasing a zipper, removing
carpet stains or scuff marks
      from a linoleum floor, unleashing
a wad of gum from a hank of hair,
      shit from a shoe, prevent snow
from slowly fattening on a windowsill.
      Anything that adhered,
was frozen, jammed, lodged, wedged,
      clogged, crammed, shoved or twisted
too snug, fastened, attached. No glue
      too super. No union
til death do us part.

I Go to the Mall for a Knife

A good knife, one that will kill
any hard root. A knife
like the knives I've seen on TV—
a man in a white chef's jacket
with wild carrot-colored hair,
hands like clay tablets, big
and biblical, dragging one thumb
along the beveled edge before
bringing it down with every pound
of his considerable weight,
splitting in half the red ruffled head
of a cabbage. I want *that* kind of knife—
maple wood haft, Kanji
characters etched on a wedge
of tempered steel. A knife worthy
of wielding. I want it to flash
like the wing of a jet plane
flying low above a chopping block
laden with garlic and peeled onions,
white knuckles smug as a many-eyed god.
I want to make a law that all knives
must be sharpened against a graphite rod
in the middle of the night when
the world can't sleep. I want to
slice the pale celery down the middle
of its spine, razor away the strings,
hold the blade to my face to check my teeth.
I want a knife that owns its shape, stealth,
sharpness and shine, a knife
worthy of its history, its name.
I want to pull it from its drawer
in the morning like I'm lifting
a thin body from a grave.

Honeymoon

We didn't have one, unless you count Paris,
20 years later, after we'd almost given up on the idea.
We'd imagined one, long nights beneath
a warm celestial sky, you growing your beard,
me in a silk turquoise robe, floating, billowing,
on a deserted beach foraging for whole sand dollars,
jellyfish washed up on the shore, their glittering insides
visible, still pulsing through flesh made of glass,
but it never happened. We had to work through
our vacations, refinance the house, find someone
to cut down the cedar that threatened to bury us
with each storm. We wanted to make up
for the wedding, or lack of one, the granite
courthouse steps, the small room with a desk,
the flimsy document stamped with a cheap gold seal.
Even then we meant to have a party on the deck,
cheese and crackers, fruit plates, sparkling
grape cider in plastic cups, our friends on the lawn
calling you the Big Kahuna, me Mrs. Dynamite,
me calling you my Sweet Dragon, you calling me
your Little Red Corvette. Instead, time found a way
to demand each minute, until one night,
after you'd gotten a small windfall in the mail,
you turned to me and said, *I'm going to take you to Paris,*
me in my ratty robe and floppy slippers, you
in your flannel PJ bottoms and black wife beater,
muting the clicker when I said "What?"
and saying it again. Then we were there,
in our 60s, standing below the dire Eiffel Tower,
its 81 stories of staircases we couldn't possibly climb,
its 73 thousand tons of puddled iron, you
taking my picture for posterity, me

kissing you beneath the pathway of arched trees,
our voices echoing against the six million skulls
embedded in the stone Catacombs, me
saying *I guess you weren't kidding,* you
taking my hand in the rain.

East Meets West

It is believed that Ho Chi Minh worked at the Carlton Hotel from 1913–1917, where he encountered the American actress Mae West.

On a summer evening, they join forces, Mae
in her gown of tears, Ho Chi Minh
in his kitchen apron stained
with duck blood and grease.

She poses before him, saying
A hard man is good to find
and he replies, *I move with all the dignity
of an ancient government official.*

She says *A man's kiss is his signature.*
He says, *When the prison doors are opened,
the real dragon will fly out.*

This is when he slides his tongue
in her mouth and they collapse
on the hotel floor like thieves,
eyes glazed as abalone.

Mae's breasts tumble from her dress
and he says, *By reading them
again and again finally I was able
to grasp the essential part.*

She touches his thigh and says
*I speak two languages: Body and English.
I've been things and seen places* . . .

The chandelier at the Carlton is still lighting up
their room in the sky, the tea leaves speaking
from the bottoms of their cups:

He says, *Love other human beings*
as you would love yourself.
She says, *I never loved another person*
the way I loved myself.

If It's the Last Thing I Do

This green-lit world in Autumn, falling
to red, to rust, Midas-touched, as fuses

are torched and rockets flare into blue
over the Pacific, two grown men squaring

off in the schoolyard, too stupid to fear,
too numbed by power to feel the air

riding over the bare skin of their soft
hands, not a lick of a good day's work

between them, TV host of sleepless nights,
childhood's parents fighting in the kitchen,

someone throwing a pot of gold against a wall.
Equal as all get out in giving in to their lesser

angels, seraphim that tumbled through
clouds of coal ash and acid rain and landed

on their feet, miraculously unscathed, but
with an unworldly ability to hate. Of late,

the trees are turning skeletal in preparation
for the shivery winter, pall of snow

laid down on the earth like a funeral cloth.
We may not live to see another spring,

another yellow summer, another flood,
another famine, another war. Maybe this

is that time when we wished them dead, our
parents, go ahead we thought as we lay

in our beds, just get it over with, and do
what you keep promising with a raised fist

will be the last goddamned thing you ever do.

Another Year on Earth

Another butt in the ashtray, another
ordinary night, but this time I unbolt the door
and walk out under it, the moon's breast full
and milky, her light chiseling the new crop
of sunflowers, their crisp yellow collars
turned earthward, their seedy eyes closed
while the bees sleep. I lean against a tree,
fix my eyes on one bright star, maybe Venus,
goddess of love and beauty, one of her days
longer than a year. She's aging so gracefully,
4.503 billion years old and she doesn't look a day
over an eon. Maybe it's because she has no moons
to tie her down like Jupiter and Saturn
who look haggard and careworn, Jupiter
with deep stretch marks and crow's feet,
Saturn surrounded by the wreckage of her life.
But Venus floats alone in her tabernacle of space,
watching TV while she lifts weights like a pro
on her living room floor, her red beauty mark
enhancing her still kissable lips. Once,
somebody said *I dare you*, and I did,
jumped off the bluff into deep seawater.
I was a teenager, dumb as they come, and when
the undertow pulled me under and spit me up
against the rocks I was sure I had completed
my last spectacular act on earth. But the boys
dove in and hauled me out so I could get as old
as I am now, almost 70, staring up at Venus
in my backyard wearing nothing
but a thin nightgown, the warm summer air
lifting it up like Marilyn Monroe's skirt, revealing
my pocked and lunar thighs.

Smash Shack

At the Smash Shack in Jacksonville, North Carolina,
in a cinder block garage, you can don a helmet
and goggles, a glass-deflecting black jumper,
face mask, gloves, and a hairnet/do-rag, pick up
a mallet or hammer, and smash, crush, break,
crack, shatter or wreck anything you want:
plates, bottles, windowpanes, crockery, mayonnaise
jars, wire-rimmed glasses, heavy ashtrays and vases
shaped like boomerangs that come flying
right back at you. You can buy the "Date Night,"
"Angry Wife" or "Armageddon" mystery box
for 10, 15 or 25 dollars, special rates for vets.
Transparent or opaque, the glass breaks the same
for bus drivers and businessmen alike, for mothers
of meth addicts, cancer patients, victims of abuse,
children of alcoholics, brain addled former
football heroes, Doctors without Borders.
Open to those of any color or creed, natives
off the rez, young Black men, the barbed-wire-scarred
Hispanic, the raped, the duped, the anorexic,
the 500 pound woman, flaming gays and lesbians,
fast food workers trying to build a union, the entire
staff of Greenpeace, ex-felons, the homeless,
children, teenagers, seniors, the comely and homely,
the wheelchair bound. What wouldn't
we break in the name of some relief, our hands
saying goodbye to candle holders and Christmas
balls, a row of old fire alarms, those horrible
elevator mirrors, fat-adding fitting room mirrors,
the inviting Cinderella mirrors framed in carved
gold hanging in Disney bathrooms. Enough
bad luck to last a century. Most of all clock faces,
glass hearts, teacups, decanters, camera lenses,

piggy banks, fishbowls, blown glass butterflies
and unicorns and if you could, every Tiffany lamp
and stained glass window in the land. Because
this is America or Japan, the Anger Room
in Houston filled with Dallas hotheads, Sarah's
Smash Shack in San Diego, the Venting Place
in Tokyo, the Rage Room in Serbia's Novi Sad
where you are offered a baseball bat to beat
a hotel TV to rubble, pummel a computer face
to pulp, at last triumphing maniacally over
the beach ball of death.

Shovel and Rake

At night I like to enter
the country of my backyard
and look up at the stars
shivering between the trees,

or higher into the kaleidoscope
yawn of the universe, all that
before so unignorably vast, listen
to the nocturnal nightjars

awake in their nest or see
a mother opossum slink past,
babies clinging to her back,
her little set of templates,

her smaller versions, her row
of replicants, her passengers
who will one day replace her,
or the lone skunk sipping

from a slick of water
where the patio dips, the tiles
sunken a bit from the last
quake, the shovel and rake

leaning like lovers against
the shed, a white T-shirt
shucked in the noonday sun
flopped over a folding chair

and flapping like a ghost,
drunk on the breeze. If we
could give ourselves
a second chance it would be

this patch of grass, this
potted plant, all the green
sucked out of them
on a moonless night,

their fronds and foliage
mere shadows in the dark,
the cedar tree a grown
woman who has stood

so long in one place
the whole world trusts her,
comes to her and shelters
in her leaves, her soft needles

that resemble feathers
as if to prove she could fly
but chooses, on a lark,
not to.

Tulip Poplar

In autumn, the tulip poplar is a tree gowned in light,
its violin-shaped leaves yellow-gold, the seed cones
cinnamon. Tall and conical, it is a tree for connoisseurs,
its branchlets reddish, lustrous smooth when young,
dark gray in adolescence, the bark maturing
to a rich furrowed brown. In spring it gathers
its inborn charisma and puts forth its finest flowers,
green-tinged buttercups, erect on their stems,
filled with orange nests of nectar. As it grows
it loses its easily broken lower branches, and so
the young will find it difficult to climb,
though cardinals perch in it to sing, and warblers
can be found playing at espionage in its crown
or staked out near the tear-shaped dollop
of a purple finch. In winter you wouldn't recognize it,
stripped of its flashy paraphernalia, poltergeist
swaying on a snowy hill, shrouded in fog,
its sullen branches sheathed in ice, its seed cones
burst into brittle Egyptian fans, but when
they finally fall the new buds emerge, tiny
red-tipped parrot beaks sipping at sunlight.
And the poplar tree goes on, building
its cottage industry of fine-grained wood
which for centuries we have cut down to make
spoons and pipe organs, cradles and coffins,
the wide floorboards of meeting houses,
churches where we have married, danced
and died. Don't ask me why
we would hang a body from such beauty,
sap wood and heart wood. We live
with its dark history, it gives us its darkest,
most bitter honey.

Enrico Salvatore Rizzo

—the final scene in Midnight Cowboy

The worst is when Ratso stops breathing and Joe won't leave him,
hugs his dead body as the Florida palms brush by the dusty window,
the bus rocking them like a cradle, its backside roped
with suitcases, a lone harmonica wheezing through the hush.

It's the scene that breaks the others open, or bends them like a bow—
the shadowy theater with its layers of smashed popcorn, the drone
behind the rolling credits, candy wrappers dropped like colorful rags
on the gum-sticky floor. Joe has let himself be unzipped by strangers,

has waited for it to be over so he can bring Ratso back a treat
from the corner store: stone-hard loaf of day-old bread, orange
juice he can drizzle like a river into a dirty glass, dribble it down
his raspy throat. Or maybe the worst part is when he says

Ratso's given name for the first time, repeating *Rico, hey Rico.*
No, it's how when the passengers all rubberneck and we watch
Joe's face slowly unfold as it relaxes into sadness, his arms around
Rico's shoulders, holding him close as a brother, as if he's still alive.

Crow Moon

Tonight is the rising of the Crow Moon,
the full moon, the Supermoon,
when the cawing of the crows signals
the end of winter, end of skeleton trees,
children with fevers, streaks of late snow
on the bricks, first crack in the frozen lake.

Crust Moon, Sap Moon, Sugar Moon,
Worm Moon, Wow! Moon. Moon
in all its windblown wildness, its long distance
somewhere, open as a marigold
in a skull's eye socket hung by a shoelace
above the chiseled hills.

And we stand below it, don't we, young
as we'll ever be, no matter how tough
our hearts, thick with scars, no matter
how nervous we are on Earth's
crumbling front porch, nothing
but a few keys in a pocket?

We stand there, looking up, wondering
which time it was when we saw this moon
before, wondering, if ever, we might
see it again, crows in the black trees
preening their wings, slicking them back
like teenagers in a 50's movie, sleek
in their leather jackets, each one
a feathered rebel without a cause.

Wild Horses

Mustangs were bred for stamina, little knock-kneed
engines. In *The Misfits* they were bred for dog food.

Marilyn Monroe was even more beautiful in black and white.
When she says she can hear her skin against her clothes

we believe her, are with her in the desert. The mustangs
crest the small hill and appear, wild-eyed, kicking up dust

and sagebrush. She watches the men hobble their legs,
preparing them for the gunshot, the daggers, the grave,

tin cans of dog food in the cupboards of every home
in America. Their liquid eyes ageless, their big hearts

pealing like cold, bronze bells. This is one role not centered
around her breasts, her chest cut open, nails in her heart.

Not a joke, nor a paradise for fantasy. It was her final movie.
They found her at home, face down, holding onto a phone.

She was born in June and died in August, near the end
of summer, white pills spilled on the rug. She always said

she liked to sleep. The men who surrounded her eased
their glasses down over their noses to look at her

in the gymnasiums of their dreams, unable to raise one barbell,
one sad cloud. Suddenly tired of their own excuses, one

held her feet, one held her shoulders, and they lifted her up.

How to Sleep

Let your mountainous forehead
with its veins of bright ore
ease down, let the deep lines
between your brows flatten,
unruffle the small muscles
below your temples, above
your jaws, let the grimace
muscles in your cheekbones
go, the weep muscles
sealing your eyes. Die into
the pillow, calm in the knowledge
that you will someday cease, soon
or late, late or soon, the song
you're made of will stop, your body
played out, the currents pulsing
through your brain drained
of their power, their purpose,
frizzling out through
your fingertips, private sparks
leaping weakly onto the sheets
where you lie breathing
and then not breathing.
Lay your head down and relax
into it: death. Accept it.
Trick yourself like this.
Hover in a veil of ethers.
Call it sleep.

Timing

Ah, timing. Woody Allen says
it's everything. I say it's nothing,
can't touch it, wear it, hold it up
between your fingers and shake it
like a napkin. Timing is what you have
when you don't have anything else,
a facility with the wine list, a joke
that hits the bull's-eye in the spongy
marrow of a funny bone. Or death,
that takes timing too, to elude,
you must bend to pick up the fork
you nervously, clumsily dropped
so the bullet that whizzed through the wall
from the shop next door where a man
of few words was holding up
a terrified clerk lost his balance
for a moment and the gun went off,
the bullet marked to end the next thought
in your roundly specific head sailing
straight through the window, shattering
the harmless glass, nicking the letter D
on the marquee across the street, a movie
you meant to see after dinner with a woman
who could become your wife, but who now
looks at you as if you are a wanted man, a man
with a foreseeable future, though not
in the way you had hoped.

Mugged by Poetry

—for Tony Hoagland, who sent me a handmade chapbook made from
old postcards called OMIGOD POETRY with a whale breaching off
the coast of New Jersey and seven of his favorite poems by various
authors typed up, taped on, and tied together with a broken shoelace.

Reading a good one can make me love the one who wrote it,
as well as the animal or element or planet or person
the poet wrote it for. I end up as I always do,
flat on my back like a drunk in the grass, loving the world.
Like right now, I'm reading a poem called "Summer"
by John Ashbery, whose poems I never much cared for,
and suddenly, in the dead of winter, *There is that sound*
like the wind / Forgetting in the branches that means
something / Nobody can translate . . . I fall in love
with that line, can actually hear it (not the line
but the wind) and it's summer again and I forget
I don't like John Ashbery poems. So I light a cigarette
and read another by Zbigniew Herbert, a poet
I've always admired but haven't read enough of, called
"To Marcus Aurelius" that begins *Good night Marcus*
put out the light / and shut the book For overhead / is raised
a gold alarm of stars . . . First of all I suddenly love
anyone with the name Zbigniew. Second of all I love
anyone who speaks in all sincerity to the dead
and by doing so brings that personage back to life,
plunging a hand through the past to flip on the light.
The astral physics of it just floors me. Third of all
is that "gold alarm of stars . . ." By now I'm a goner,
and even though I have to get up tomorrow at 6 am
I forge ahead and read "God's Justice" by Anne Carson,
another whose poems I'm not overly fond of
but don't actively disdain. I keep reading one line

over and over, hovering above it like a speckled starling
spying on the dragonfly with *turquoise dots all down its back
like Lauren Bacall.* Like Lauren Bacall!! Well hell,
I could do this all night. I could be in love like this
for the rest of my life, with everything in the expanding
universe and whatever else might be beyond it
that we can't grind a lens big enough to see. I light up
another smoke, maybe the one that will kill me,
and go outside to listen to the moon scalding
the iced trees. What, I ask you, will become of me?

Spoleto

I remember Italy for the water
falling from the mouths
of stone lions, the liquid
birdsong of sparrows, arias
floating from the open doors
of the Cathedral, so beautiful
you wanted to collapse
on the cobblestones
and crawl toward the sound,
your palms embedded
with 2000 year old gravel.
I remember biting into
a Pinova apple, honey sweet,
crisp as winter, mosaics
set in the walls, every window
flung open to the breeze,
the breeze scented with vanilla
from the *Pasticceria*. It was so human:
the buzzing cafés and terraces,
the vendors, dogs and children
and doves in the street, the wooden
wheels of painted carts, the sun
surrendering to the shade
of red and green umbrellas,
their taut wire ribs. Even
the ugliest baby in a carriage,
its face still scrunched
from the womb, blinked
its dark eyes up at you
and banged its small fists
against its fat cherub thighs.
When we left I felt banished,
bereft that I couldn't take

it with me, the little bell
that tinkled when we stepped in
and the cashier pointed
to an empty tiled table
where I first learned the word
for ice cream was *gelato*,
and the word for *gelato* with
a shot of espresso is *affogato*
al caffee, dessert of the angels
that slipped over our tongues
and down our throats
like a landslide, a flavor
we would taste all day
as we walked the ungodly
hot streets, wobbling along
the uneven roads, our shirts
stuck to our chests with sweat,
smelling of genoa sausage, our breath
of onions and garlic, the olive oil
stain on my best silk blouse
I could never get out.

Garage Band

—for my brother, Jack

My brother had one, my boyfriend.
Every man I have loved loved music.
Each song a pearl threaded onto a necklace
I have worn all my life. I see them,
sitting on crates, guitars strapped
over their chests, tools hung
from rusty nails behind their heads,
oil stains at their feet. A drumbeat
so loud every mirror in the house
shook, each window a prism
of fragile light. Was I sixteen
when I first heard them? Saw them
trapped in the boxed garage surrounded
by oily engine parts, coiled hoses,
shovels leaning against battered trash bins,
the air smelling of gas and dust
and stale cigarettes? My brother's fingers
shuttled across the organ keys,
all of them singing a cover of Jimi's
"Are You Experienced?", a guitar string
strangled toward heaven, a compass
crushed under the bass drum's pedal,
a cousin refusing to go to war, a lapse
in the fabric of time. My life
has been blessed by these visits
glimpsed through the gauze of the past.
And weren't they what we deserved?
Their music booming down
the suburban streets, reminding us

who we were and who we could be,
their beauty and truth, their youth
and exuberance, crashing into
the chronic silence of our lives.

Stay here

don't look back, remain
in the present, don't remember
how you were born, the waters
breaking away from you, untwisted
from the womb, how you were
held, mid-air in a stranger's hands,
set down on a pillow, the blood
wiped from your eyes two stones
that gazed, uncomprehending,
into the corner of a white room,
the ceiling like a floor you would
one day crawl across, walk across,
one day sit facing in a chair, punishment
for hitting your four year old brother
the grower below you would one day
birth, along with your sisters you have
also hit or touched with a toy wand
to turn into pumpkins or princesses,
or pull their hair or brush it, strumming
each gold filament like a harp. You curled
idle, silent, and solitary in that dark
for so long, waiting to cross the border
into the new world, to be released
into your human form, the one who
could choose to use your new body
however you liked, as weapon
or whisper, as companion or cudgel,
agent of brutality or balm. I had to learn
to be quiet again, to hold onto the before
when all I wanted was to be allowed
into the kingdom of day and night,

seasons and music, which was
everywhere, muffled as it was,
and the silence that followed after.

Valentine

Once we stood on a bridge over
a lime-green pond, having left
the fallen starling we saved and raised
as our own, the feathered child
we would never have,
at the bird sanctuary.
For almost a year we had prepared
her meals over the sink, a mush
of dry cat food, as she stood
on our shoulders and ate
from the end of a chopstick.
Later we scratched in the dirt
and pulled up a worm
or offered her a dead moth
caught between the screen
and the sill. Whole afternoons
watching her try her wings
until she could fly from lamp
to bookcase, from chair back
to hat rack. We worshiped her,
this weightless body
of hollow bones, even
the tiny coils of her bowels, curls
of guano on the Ficus leaves.
When she bathed in a bowl
on the counter top, we praised her.
At night she slept on our chests
beneath a cathedral of palms
as we watched TV, trilling
like a tiny piano through her dreams.
The sanctuary had a weathercock
that spun slowly on the breeze,
cages big as houses filled

with more of her kind, and other
homeless creatures they
would one day release
in protective flocks
after having learned to follow
and forage, to fly and nest.
It was a quiet death we held
between us, and I think
he heard the blade pass through
my heart before I began to cry,
my head on the railing, my ear
pressed to my ticking watch.
Maybe every crossing guides us.
He helped me over the bridge
and into the car and we drove
through the hills, and from then
on, every starling we saw
in a parking lot could be her.

Fig

Now that I'm 70 I'm trying to stay
focused on my feet, trying not to
trip so I won't break a hip, end up

in a hospital surrounded by a swarm
of nurses and germs, a plastic container
of apple sauce, a juice box of prunes,

bleachy blankets thin as a wish.
I don't want to die like this, a kingdom
of white walls, machines beeping

beside me, saints appearing in my
peripheral vision offering to escort me
to the final door. I want to die bent

to the tide, lifting a shell to my ear
or listening to the duende blues
on an old record player, tapping the arm

to the next groove when it skips.
I don't mind becoming fertilizer, that
honorable substance. It's not the darkness

I fear. It's the bright lights, needles
and ether, the P.A. system and the air-
conditioned air. I want to die like

a criminal in my own provenance,
eating the last stolen fig.

My Husband Explains the Equinox

standing naked in the living room
at 8 am, spreading his arms
like da Vinci's Vitruvian Man,
one finger pointed at the window,
the other toward the back door.

This is true east and true west,
and today, and today only, (as if
it's a sale on the loudspeaker
at Walmart), the sun rises and sets
the same for everyone in the world.

Overwhelmed by the weight
of this celestial fact, he straightens
his spine and says: *Of course*
this is not to minimize
the importance of the Solstice.

(All this, before my second cup of coffee.)

To diss the Solstice, he adds, gazing down at his cock,
you'd have to be a fool.

The Cup

Shells or hollowed-out stones, curved bones.
Woven leaves, shaped clay, glazed and fired.
Tin, porcelain, glass, pale ceramic, paper or plastic.

The cup, we are told, holds on, invented by no one,
made to contain and appease: water, tea, coffee,
hot chocolate or pudding, carrot soup, a carnival

of uses. One handled, two handled, painted or plain.
There is no one, I imagine, who is against the cup,
even the unmatched cup alone in its namesake

cupboard, its twin having fallen with a great noise
to the floor in shards and stars. A grandmother
somewhere in time packed her cups in a suitcase,

carried them into the new world on a ship, the frosted
waves clashing and shattering under the tinfoil moon.
Not one of her packed cups cracked. When she died

she left them to her daughter who swaddled them
in newsprint, her hands shaking as she put them away,
the same hands she cupped around her mother's face,

drinking her in before the last wave washed her away.

Praise

She sat on the lawn like
a truck up on blocks, naked
as a jaybird, screaming
like a banshee, cursing
like a sailor way down
in the San Diego dumps.
She was flapping her arms
like a flightless bird,
a Chaplinesque dandy,
pumped up on her own
concoction of OxyContin
and Vicodin, street codeine
and speed, grass blade
stains on the caps
of her knees, dirt clods
flattened under her heels,
armpits unshaven,
blonde-thatched mons—
her bone of contention,
salt in her wound—
until the cops arrive
with a scratchy blanket
and zip-tie cuffs, more
moves now than a bowl
of Jell-O, a jar of bees,
as the cops—can't
stop 'em, can commit a crime
without 'em—grab a hank
of her steal your thunder
hair, and she's ready
for the funny farm to drive her
up a wall, trim her sails, go at her
with a hammer and tongs, turn

the tables and bend her over
backwards, a little more
than she bargained for
this mad woman pissing
her mad woman's red piss.
Now her head's a pummel
beating up the back seat
as the cops take off their hats
and mop their brows, ask me
who the hell she is and I say
She's my sister so you
better be careful, this shit
runs in the blood.

Snow

It wasn't snowing, and then it was,
like death, like my sister's texts
that just stopped: *I'm in the hospital*
then a phone call: *We did everything*

we could: endocarditis, valve leakage,
her heart on heroin. She wasn't addicted

and then she was, on and off, for years
she and her daughter, my niece, living
on the streets, every few weeks a phone call:
we need a motel room, food. Once we ordered them
a pizza from the other coast where we had moved
to get away from them, though we couldn't

quite quit them, family, addicted, a feeling,
a rush of guilt, the wrong address, we never knew
where the pizza went. She was a statistic,
one of the twelve-fold increase, they must have
folded her clothes, dropped them in a bag
with her purse, her phone, what little

she had left, though the woman's shelter
had no record, though they had other bags
she'd filled with nothing more than rags:
a wealth of sweatpants, unraveled sweaters,
a box of makeup and a toothless comb, picture
her grandchild had scribbled in with magic marker:

a parrot in a cage, its folded wings bled through
to the other side. I understand how it happened,
but it doesn't matter, it was inevitable, unavoidable,
if anyone of us was going to fall prey it was her,
middle child of too many to count, not enough
love to go around. I was in New York, it was

snowing, Michael Moore was onstage
in front of an American flag when the phone
buzzed, went to the stairwell where I was told,
alone on the metal steps, *She's gone*, sobbing
when a voice from a dark doorway asked
Are you alright? a guard in his booth,

My sister died. He handed me a box
of Kleenex and closed the door, it seemed,
to give me privacy. Back in the cab I sat
between my girlfriends, hip to hip,
like sisters, an arm around each shoulder,
all night we had been laughing and then

we weren't, they asked me questions
and then they stopped and we rode on
into the snow, powder, black tar, brown
sugar, junk, scag, skunk, dragon, china white.
Snow. Then the cabbie turned right and eased
through a slew of pedestrians, a sea of coats

and gloves, wool scarves, faces hidden
beneath hats, it was like the whole country
was out on night patrol, trudging forward
stolidly, seriously, like we had to plow our way
through it, keep our heads down, keep going.

Waitress

When I was young and had to rise at 5 am
I did not look at the lamplight slicing
through the blinds and say: Once again
I have survived the night. I did not raise
my two hands to my face and whisper:
This is the miracle of my flesh. I walked
toward the cold water waiting to be released
and turned the tap so I could listen to it
thrash through the rusted pipes.
I cupped my palms and thought of nothing.

I dressed in my blue uniform and went to work.
I served the public, looked down on its
balding skulls, the knitted shawls draped
over its cancerous shoulders, and took its orders,
wrote *up* or *easy* or *scrambled* or *poached*
in the yellow pads' margins and stabbed it through
the tip of the fry cook's deadly planchette.

Those days I barely had a pulse. The manager
had vodka for breakfast, the busboys hid behind
the bleach boxes from the immigration cops,
and the head waitress took ten percent
of our tips and stuffed them in her pocket
with her cigarettes and lipstick. My feet
hurt. I balanced the meatloaf-laden trays.
Even the tips of my fingers ached.

I thought of nothing except sleep, a TV set's
flickering cathode gleam washing over me,
baptizing my greasy body in its watery light.
And money, slipping the tassel of my coin purse
aside, opening the silver clasp, staring deep
into that dark sacrificial abyss.

What can I say about that time, those years
I leaned over the rickety balcony on my break
smoking my last saved butt?
It was sheer bad luck when I picked up
the glass coffee pot and spun around
to pour another cup. All I could think
as it shattered was how it was the same size
and shape as the customer's head. And this is why
I don't believe in accidents, the grainy dregs
running like sludge down his thin tie
and pin-stripe shirt like they were channels
riven for just this purpose.

It wasn't my fault. I know that. But what, really,
was the hurry? I dabbed at his belly with a napkin.
He didn't have a cut on him (physics) and only
his earlobe was burned. But my last day there
was the first day I looked up as I walked, the trees
shimmering green lanterns under the Prussian blue
particulate sky, sun streaming between my fingers
as I waved at the bus, running, breathing hard, thinking:
This is the grand phenomenon of my body. This thirst
is mine. This is my one and only life.

Lake Havasu

Man-made, bejesus hot, patches of sand turned to glass.
Home of Iron Mountain and McCulloch chain saws.

London Bridge, disassembled, shipped, reassembled.
The white sturgeon stocked, found dead, some lost,
hiding in the depths of Parker Dam. Fifty year old
monsters, maybe twenty feet long. Lake named

for the Mojave word for blue. *Havasu. Havasu.*
What we called the sky on largemouth bass days,

striped bass nights, carp, catfish, crappie, razorback,
turtles, stocked, caught, restocked. I stood waist deep
in that dammed blue, and I was beautiful, a life saver
resting on my young hips, childless, oblivious

to politics, to the life carted in and dumped
into the cauldron I swam through, going under,

gliding along the cool sand like a human fish,
white bikini-ed shark flashing my blind side.
We heard a woman died, face down in the sand,
drunk on a 125 degree day. That night we slept

on dampened sheets, a hotel ice bucket on the
bedside table. We sucked the cubes round, slid

the beveled edges down our thighs and spines,
let them melt to pools in the small caves
below our sternums. While you slept beside me
I thought of that woman, her body one long

third degree burn, sweating and turning
under a largo moon, the TV on: seven dead

from Tylenol, the etched black wedge of the
Vietnam Memorial, the Commodore Computer
unveiled, the first artificial heart.

The Lyre

They say Nero fiddled while Rome burned, though
of course there were no fiddles, and the violin
was still curled like a secret inside the trees, waiting to be
cesareaned by Amati, carved from ebony, maple and spruce,
the most famous and oldest among them, the most
pristine, being "Le Messie" or the "Salabue"
made by Antonio Stradivari in 1717, and never used,
hung like a cadaver in the Ashmolean Museum.

It was April 20th, 2010 when the oil began pumping
into the Gulf of Mexico. We watched the news
on our flat screens and iPads. We watched
ripe beds of kelp wash up on the beige sand,
gloved hands scrubbing the blackened beaks
of pelicans, that collapsible bird that's been around
for 30 thousand years. We watched the last
great buckets of gray shrimp poured and weighed

like grain, and the faces of fishermen give way.
We saw the trawlers head out, dragging
their long booms, capturing little acres of oil,
we saw the sheen, like an old silver mirror,
we saw fire on the water—so real
we could almost smell the waxy black plumes.
Some of us sang. Some of us stood racked
with fear. Most of us went about the business

of our day, discussing the price of gas, buying
lottery tickets at the supermarket, a bag of chips.
Mostly, we didn't think about it. Who could?
Because it was so deep under the water, out of view.
It's not like the city itself was burning or even
the forest around the city. Therefore we woke

and worked or looked for work, so many of us
out of work by then, and after work we walked

to the park with our children and friends, barbecued
through the long weekend, Memorial Day, the day
we once set aside to commemorate the Union dead
in the Civil War, though now we try not to think of it
as the Civil War because it's too confusing—
The Greys. The Blues. Just the war dead in general
was how we took care of that. If this was the end
of the world as we knew it, we didn't know it.

We were a large country, a country that ran on luck,
and the year had been both unseasonably warm
and unreasonably cool. We didn't know
what to do. But yes, some of us sang.

Joy

Even when the gods have driven you
from your home, your friends, the tree
you planted brought down by storm,
drought, chain saw, beetles, even

when you've been scrubbed
hollow by confusion, loss,
accept joy, those unbidden
moments of surcease,

the quiet unfolding
around your shoulders
like a shawl, the warmth
that doesn't turn to burning.

When the itch has stopped, the cough,
the throb, the heart's steady beat
resumed, the barn door

open to the shade, the horse inside
waiting for your touch, apple
in your pocket pocked, riddled

the last to fall, the season
done. As you would accept
air into your lungs, without
thinking, not counting

each breath. As you accepted
the earth the first time you stood
up on it and it held you, how it was

just there, a solid miracle,
gravity something you would
learn about only later
and still be amazed.

I Dare You

It's autumn, and we're getting rid
of books, getting ready to retire,
to move some place smaller, more
manageable. We're living in reverse,
age-proofing the new house, nothing
on the floors to trip over, no hindrances
to the slowed mechanisms of our bodies,
a small table for two. Our world is
shrinking, our closets mostly empty,
gone the tight skirts and dancing shoes,
the bells and whistles. Now, when
someone comes to visit and admires
our complete works of Shakespeare,
the hawk feather in the open dictionary,
the iron angel on a shelf, we say
take them. This is the most important
time of all, the age of divestment,
knowing what we leave behind is
like the fragrance of blossoming trees
that grows stronger after
you've passed them, breathing
them in for a moment before
breathing them out. An ordinary
Tuesday when one of you says
I dare you, and the other one
just laughs.

I Watch My Neighbor Watch Porn through the Kitchen Window

while I wash the dishes, the back of his head propped
along the sofa's curved and tufted rim, his hand
caressing a glass of black wine. I can make out the shapes
of the woman, blurred breast, flash of thigh, as I scrape
grease into a coffee can, wipe the pan with a paper towel.
He's married with a new baby, the light upstairs dimming
each time she rocks, probably cooing and fawning
as a mother does, while her husband stares at the screen
and takes a drink, looking up at the ceiling every once
in a while, his gaze almost wistful, as if listening
for angels, before lowering his head and going back
to his work. What are the limits of marriage? The plot
is hilarious, an elegant office, the woman in a judicial robe
holding a gavel, the man cowering in a dog collar waiting
for the fist of justice to fall, or maybe she's quoting
the Bible: *collect ye not vessels of wine but crates of tears.*
When the light upstairs goes off and his wife appears,
he slides over so she can sit down, puts his arm around her,
rests his head on her shoulder, and I go on watching, washing
bowls and spoons, placing each one gently in the rack.

Jalopy

Under the blown-out stars
sounds the lone horn
of the Cucaracha car

the slow rolling music box
of the ice cream truck
rising from the muck

Trumpet vine
ball of twine
yours/mine . . .

Dig yourself out
from your house
in the ground

flick the dimes
off your eyes
and come dance with me

through the streets, your feet
between sidewalk cracks
Twist my back low

and bop with a ghost
my holy host
stop with me beneath

the stop sign
its red hexagon
a heart chopped down

like a stolen car
parked along the curb
loading and unloading

the gun in your pocket
Let's jump off the dock
unlock the flame inside us

float over to the waters
of Mexico, heave ho
heave into me, weave

me into the singing
of the ringing phone
alone on the pier

swim into the going-gone
sun, our bodies turning rose
as night comes on

smother my wet face
with underwater kisses
I miss you so much

I could drown.

Moon Ghazal

I can't remember the first time I saw it, seems it was
always there, even with me in the womb, the moon.

It must have been night, above the ocean, making a path
on the waves, gilded invitation, the parchment moon.

Or the day moon, see-through-y wafer over desert, caught
in the arms of Saguaro, thin-skinned, heart-stuck moon.

Blue as new milk, aquarium water, Mexican tiles, blue
as fingertips in the cold, nailbeds quick-blue arcs, half-moons.

How I felt when I saw my first grown boy, round-eyed,
all sinew and muscle, his calves, his biceps, plump as moons.

Buttons, doorknobs, volleyballs, clocks, egg yolk, orange
slice, violet iris, our planet a pupil, mote in the eye of the moon.

The cell inside me splitting and splitting, worm of the fetus,
tadpole, the glazed orb of the eye, my belly taut as the moon.

The blood-streaked moon of her head pushing through, moons
of the faces above me, urging me, pulling, promising the moon.

There are earthquakes on the moon, not geologically dead, still
acting like a planet: upheaval, turmoil, shaking her head, the moon.

When I see the earth of you I still feel moon-quakes, even now, after
so many moons, my round breasts swoon, your fingertips small moons.

My body had become a field,

my nipple
a stone, as I sat at the window nursing
my daughter, loving her hunger, snatching
at my breast the way a flower swallows
the sun, gulping at that other fiery
life-giving rock in space, its milky rays,
her budded tongue, her bid
for existence. I loved her
persistence, the tower of my body
hovering above her, the clock
of my face bearing its tracks
of laughter and sadness, my eyes
on tip-toe watching her eyes
as they closed over her ecstasy,
unashamed, listened to her mantra
of satisfied sips until she was sated,
until she had walked from one end
of a bridge to the other, over
her river of need and into the bright
forest of sleep, my heart loud
in its beating, her smaller heart
picking up the rhythm, the window
propped open to the oncoming day.

Spring

The birds are going, the bees are almost gone—
lost habitat, hive collapse, cell and nest,
the earth bereft, the world devoid of song.

We work to right the blight, the nights so long,
the tangled woods won't answer our request.
The birds are going, the bees have almost gone.

The birds are arrows, the bees are never wrong.
They make their loops and lassos as they must.
They sleep inside themselves but never rest.
The birds are singing, the bees all buzz and hum.

They love their dusty mothers, seed and pollen clung
to beak and leg, they rock the bitter hour, the moon crests.
The birds are crying out, the bees are close to gone.

To make this world enough they make another one
built of wings and eyes, hollow bones, downy breasts.
They leave their gauzy ghost trails on the sky's blue chest.
The birds are going, the bees are almost gone.

The smallest park in America

is dedicated to a poet, maybe
five people can stand up in it
which is enough warm bodies
for most poetry readings. Most
poetry readings are given at
dusk, the darkest part of twilight,
a poetic word if there ever was
one. The time right before Orion
rises in the east, a time when
all five poets look up and sing
their verses to his belt. There
is always a vase of just-cut
flowers dying in a narrow
vase set upon a skinny, wobbly
lectern, a squat glass of water
some poets replace with vodka,
maybe a splash of bitters.
Their poems are peeled
in layers like onion skins and
someone always cries mineral
tears that fall onto patches
of grass below from which
a staircase grows, winding
in a spiral into the crowns
of trees above, dislodging
hazel nuts everyone then
cracks with their poet-
loving teeth, grinding down
the mealy meat. After many
long distances and a boat
load of words, the poetry
reading ends, first to silence,
then to quiet applause,

at which point someone
bends down and unlatches
the shin-high gate and they
parade out the door made
of any weather and into
the dark hallways of evening
to search for their cars.
They stand for a moment
under the stars, remembering
what it was like to be held
gently in a lion's open mouth.

Moonflaw

The rivers of my brain
flow east and west,
or if I stand on my head
they pour onto the floor.

Essex England has a town
called Braintree, the River
Brain runs through it,
deep meander that joins

the Blackwater near Witham.
With whom? I asked, back
when I had a boyfriend
who used to say he just

"went out." What he meant,
of course, was that his brain's
convolutions, made up of sulci
(the creases) and gyri (the ridges)

told him he needed a beer.
The more we laugh, the more
we etch lines into our faces.
Charles Reznikoff says:

The fingers of your thoughts
are molding your face
ceaselessly. Dolphins
have more creases than

humans, which must mean
they laugh, even in their sleep.

The creases in the brain
are called "axions."

The crease in your butt
is called the intergluteal cleft.
Between your nose and lip:
the philtrum. The underside

of your kneecap is called
the patella. Deep knee bends
can lead to wear and tear
and cause arthritis.
The muscles that cause
crow's feet are the
orbicularis oculi.
Happiness flaws

our lives. Only
dogs, cats, monkeys
and the aforementioned
dolphins have brain folds.

Rats, for instance,
still possess a primitive,
flat, unfolded brain.
Brain creases

increase the available
surface area, like the fins
of car radiators,
a highly evolved trait

which allows us to lie
and know we are being

lied to, and still be happy,
still laugh in our sleep,

a flaw that's not quite
a flaw.

Blossom

What is a wound but a flower
dying on its descent to the earth,
bag of scent filled with war, forest,
torches, some trouble that befell
now over and done. A wound is a fire
sinking into itself. The tinder serves
only so long, the log holds on
and still it gives up, collapses
into its bed of ashes and sand. I burned
my hand cooking over a stove's low flame,
that flame now alive under my skin,
the smell not unpleasant, the wound
beautiful as a full-blown peony.
Say goodbye to disaster. Shake hands
with the unknown, what becomes
of us once we've been torn apart
and returned to our future, naked
and small, sewn back together
scar by scar.

Bedtime Stories

I like falling asleep to *Ancient Aliens*, watching
those flickering *X-File* lights tessellating
through the forest, the glowing disks, triangles,
and long metal lozenges—the three basic shapes
of UFOs—caught on cameras and wobbly videos.

I love the secret of the pyramids, how the man
in a lab coat, scientist of renown, asks
How the heck did they do it? What kind of
celestial saw did they use? How did they transport
them from one island to another? What kind of angels
are carved into the chapels of massive stone?

I like listening to the hum of space gears
and distant stars, like tinnitus in a tin cup,
the sand turned to glass where the ship
touched down on their rotating bands
of turquoise lights. I love the child-like
drawings of those who've been abducted,
the ovoid heads on spider-like bodies,
their eyes translucent capsules of vitamin B-12,

mouthless, earless, sexless creatures
tasked with human examination, prodding
and pulsing above the darkly vaginal ones,
flowering penises that must confound them
as much as they confound us, bathed
in a shower of curiosity and confusion
beneath the incandescent dome.

Episode after episode they arrive and depart,
each show more impossible and vaguely
probable than the last, until the night
finally takes me into the sweet release
of sleep and I doze off in the TV's
cathode beam, its glimmer and glint,
its gleam and flare as I fall up into space
made of nothing but light and time, formless
and flailing, an alien to my waking life.

I Never Wanted to Die

It's the best part of the day, morning light sliding
down rooftops, treetops, the birds pulling themselves
up out of whatever stupor darkened their wings,
night still in their throats.
I never wanted to die. Even when those I loved
died around me, away from me, beyond me.
My life was never in question, if for no other reason
than I wanted to wake up and see what happened next.
And I continue to want to open like that, like the flowers
who lift their heavy heads as the hills outside the window
flare gold for a moment before they turn
on their sides and bare their creased backs.
Even the cut flowers in a jar of water lift
their soon to be dead heads and open
their eyes, even they want a few more sips,
to dwell here, in paradise, a few days longer.

Sundays

Our mother would make two ponytails
on either side of our heads with red rubber bands,
so tight our ears ached, then dip a comb
in a glass of water and run it through
our thin blonde hair until it wept,
then lift her index finger and rake
the wet hair around it before she slid
it out leaving a long damp curl.
If we squirmed, and we did, she would snap
the wet comb off our bare arms
which blazed with scored red lines.
We had to sit still while our curls dried,
straight in our chairs in our matching
pink dresses, our white, white socks,
our black patent leather shoes, staring
at the paint-by-number framed
on the wall: a barn, a fence, cows stranded
on a patch of green in the distance.
I studied the paint-by-number clouds
drooping over the church steeple
on the yellow hill, a thin white, so thin
I could see the numbers through them:
zero, zero, zero,
as if God had given everything in the world
a value and the poor clouds had none,
made as they were of vapor, mere
water and air, good for little but gazing at
as they changed shape, each new one
worthless as the last.

Peach

I kneel to the ground fall peach
its russet belly, its honey streaks,
touch its new tough skin, run my thumb
along its deep, sexy cleft. I pluck another
from a low branch, tug it down into
captivity like an animal caught
in a bramble, scooped into my arms
that open to return it to the wide field
of my cutting board where I lift
the knife, slice around the stony pit,
its purple edges bleeding into the gold flesh
in a starburst, and like a star
becoming into silence, miniscule
pulse of living light from this distance,
has been making itself over and over
from the fire within it, like the sound hole
of a violin that welcomes any dark music.
To think we can eat a sunset,
convicted, as we are, to the mud
of this earth, knees dark with dirt, hands
sticky with essence, to think I too
am here in this cleft body, a being
split into parts and seamed back
together, swollen with desire,
hungry for the sun.

Life on Earth

The odds are we should never have been born.
Not one of us. Not one in 400 trillion to be
exact. Only one among the 250 million
released in a flood of semen that glides
like a glassine limousine filled with tadpoles
of possible people, one of whom may
or may not be you, a being made of water
and blood, a creature with eyeballs and limbs
that end in fists, a you with all your particular
perfumes, the chords of your sinewy legs
singing as they form, your organs humming
and buzzing with new life, moonbeams
lighting up your brain's gray coils,
the exquisite hills of your face, the human
toy your mother longs for, your father
yearns to hold, the unmistakable you
who will take your first breath, your first
step, bang a copper pot with a wooden spoon,
trace the lichen growing on a boulder you climb
to see the wild expanse of a field, the one
whose heart will yield to the yellow forsythia
named after William Forsyth—not the American
actor with piercing blue eyes, but the Scottish
botanist who discovered the buttery bells
on a highland hillside blooming
to beat the band, zigzagging down
an unknown Scottish slope. And those
are only a few of the things
you will one day know, slowly chipping away
at your ignorance and doubt, you
who were born from ashes and will return
to ash. When you think you might be

through with this body and soul, look down
at an anthill or up at the stars, remember
your gambler chances, the bounty
of good luck you were born for.

Acknowledgments

"In Any Event," *Raleigh Review*

"The Thermopolium," AQR

"Psalm," *Ploughshares*

"The Optimism of French Toast," *Résonance*

"Spirit Level," "Winter Brother," "My Husband Explains the Equinox," "Singer," "Timing," APR

"Ode to the Territory," "Salt," "Joy," "Enrico Salvatore Rizzo," *Southampton Review*

"Third Rock from the Sun," Poem-a-Day, Academy of American Poets

"I'll Be Here on My Back Porch," *New York Quarterly*, *Tiferet Journal*

"Bisquick," *Chicago Quarterly Review*

"Snow," *Prairie Schooner*

"I Go to the Mall for a Knife," *Cortland Review*

"East Meets West," *Explosion-Proof*

"If It's the Last Thing I Do," *Rattle*: Poets Respond

"Smash Shack," *American Journal of Poetry*

"Shovel and Rake," "Fig," "Spoleto," *Five Points*

"Tulip Poplar," "Honeymoon," *Tin House*

"Crow Moon," *Sierra*

"Valentine," *Night Heron Barks*

"How to Sleep," *River Styx*, reprinted on *Poetry Daily*

"Another Year on Earth," *I Wanna Be Loved by You*, Marilyn Monroe anthology

"Mugged by Poetry," *Cortland Review*

"Peach," "Moon Ghazal," "Wild Horses," *Poetry*

"The Cup," *Ex/Post*

"Praise," *High Desert Journal*

"Waitress," *Once Was Blip*

"Lake Havasu," Poem-a-Day, Academy of American Poets

"The Lyre," *Orion*

"Joy," *Plume*

"Life on Earth," *The Atlantic*

"Blossom," Poem-a-Day, Academy of American Poets

"The smallest park in America," *Harvard Review*

"I Never Wanted to Die," Poem-a-Day, Academy of American Poets

"Moonflaw," "I Watch My Neighbor Watch Porn through the Kitchen Window," *Plume*

"Moon Ghazal" was featured on Poem-a-Day, Academy of America Poets

Gratitude:

Thank you to everyone in my life who helped me to become a poet: my family, my friends, my daughter and husband, and Joel Rosen. Thank you to my colleagues and the poets in my life. And to the Sunday and Monday Poetry groups who zoomed with me throughout the pandemic and beyond, without whom this book would not have been possible. Thank you to the magazines that first published these poems. Gratitude is also due Jill Bialosky, Drew Weitman, and those at W. W. Norton who took such care in creating this book. Also to Vaughan Fielder of the Field Office Agency for her attentiveness and grace. Thank you to the Desert Rat Residency and the Academy of American Poets. And thank you to my mother, who gave me this life on earth.

Notes

"In Any Event" was included in the chapbook SALT, published by the Field Office. It was later made into a broadside by *Poets for Science*, a participatory exhibit exploring the connection between science and poetry, curated by Jane Hirshfield.

"The Thermopolium" is a winner of the 2023 Pushcart Prize in Poetry.

It was also showcased in *Pièces de Résistance*: Craft Conversation: FACTS INTO POEMS. Jane Hirshfield and I discussed our poems that emerged from the same factual source as well as our craft approach to writing those poems, https://www.youtube.com/watch?v=3UZgJwknlrw.

"The Optimism of French Toast": *Résonance* publishes writing about the Franco American communities of the United States, edited by its editorial board in Orono, Maine, under the aegis of the Franco American Programs of the University of Maine. The song "Acadian Driftwood" by The Band alludes to and mostly adheres to the historical facts, though Robertson takes poetic license when he says the Seven Years War (called the French Indian War in the United States) "was over." It had only just begun in 1756. My family is of Acadian French descent and when I was a child I read the poem "Evangeline: A Tale of Acadie," a book-length poem about the "ethnic cleansing" of the French by Henry Wadsworth Longfellow. Longfellow was born in Maine, home to many Acadian French. Robertson (also Acadian French) says the poem inspired his song.

"The smallest park in America": Mill Ends Park is a tiny urban park consisting of one tree, located in the median strip of SW Naito Parkway in downtown Portland, Oregon. The park is a small circle 2 feet across, with a total area of 452 square inches. It is the smallest park in the world, according to the Guinness Book of Records, which first granted it this recognition in 1971.

"Tulip Poplar" alludes to these lines from the Billie Holiday song "Strange Fruit":

Black bodies swinging in the southern breeze
Strange fruit hanging from the poplar trees

The poplar tree, also known as Liriodendron tulipifera or the tulip tree, is the state tree of Tennessee, which is also the state where the Ku Klux Klan originated.

"The Lyre": Deepwater Horizon oil spill, also called Gulf of Mexico oil spill, largest marine oil spill in history, caused by an April 20, 2010 explosion on the Deepwater Horizon oil rig—located in the Gulf of Mexico approximately 41 miles (66 km) off the coast of Louisiana— and its subsequent sinking on April 22. —Britannica: https://www .britannica.com/event/Deepwater-Horizon-oil-spill

"Lake Havasu": White sturgeon were stocked in Lake Havasu in 1967 and 1968 from stock obtained from San Pablo Bay, California. While some dead sturgeon were found downstream from Havasu (probably killed during passage over dams), living fish have not been recorded, but may still exist along the southern end of Lake Havasu near Parker Dam. —Wiki

"Smash Shack": The origin of rage rooms, also known as smash or anger rooms, can be traced back to Japan in 2008. The launch of the Venting Place in Tokyo coincided with Japan's economy falling into a recession and it offered locals a place where they could relieve stress by smashing dishes and throwing plates.

"If It's the Last Thing I Do": was written for *Rattle*, Poets Respond in October 2017. At the time, I noted, "I wrote this poem after reading what Russian foreign minister Sergei Lavrov told reporters at the United Nations last week: 'We have to calm down the hot heads. We continue to strive for the reasonable and not the emotional approach . . . of the kindergarten fight between children.'"